SUCCESS

by Janet McDonnell
illustrated by Linda Hohag
and Lori Jacobson

BASALT REGIONAL LIBRARY
99 MIDLAND AVENUE
BASALT CO 81621-8305

THE CHILD'S WORLD

Mankato, MN 56001

'Tis a lesson you should heed,

Try, try again;

If at first you don't succeed,

Try, try again.

— T. H. Palmer
Try, Try Again

Library of Congress Cataloging in Publication Data

McDonnell, Janet, 1962-
    Success.

    (What is it?)
    Summary: Describes success and how it can be
achieved in everyday life.
    1. Success—Juvenile literature.   2. Children—
Conduct of life.   [1. Success]   I. Hohag, Linda, ill.
II. Title.   III. Series.
BJ1611.2.H65   1988   646.7   88-4348
ISBN 0-89565-376-1

© 1988 The Child's World, Inc.
All rights reserved. Printed in U.S.A.

What is success? When you try
very hard and are finally able to
say, "I did it!"—that's success.

Success is finishing that fifty-
piece puzzle with all the blue-
sky pieces.

And it's painting a picture that
makes you happy and proud.

Winning an award for the
Halloween costume that you
and Mom made, that's success!

Success is teaching your little
sister the alphabet . . .

learning how to whistle . . .

and making it all the way
across the monkey bars.

13

Success is practicing a song for
the Christmas program over and
over . . .

and then singing it the best you
can on the night of the program.

When you save your allowance
week after week, and finally
have enough money to buy a
new truck, that's success!

Success is finding your friend
in hide-and-go-seek.

And it's hiding so well that
your friend can't find you!

Success is finding a way to have
fun on a rainy day.

Success is finding out that the
boat you and Dad built really
does float!

And when Mom teaches you to make brownies, and everyone says, "Delicious!"—that's success.

When you can open a book and
say, "I can read it myself, Mom,"
that's success.

You have to try some things,
like riding a bike, again and
again before . . .

you are successful!

Success is reaching a goal. It's finishing a task. It's doing the best you can do.

Can you think of other ways to
be successful?

BASALT REGIONAL LIBRARY
99 MIDLAND AVENUE
BASALT CO 81621-8305